Interactive Press
Pentimento

Daniel Ionita, born in Bucharest, Romania, teaches Organisational Improvement, part-time, at the University of Technology, Sydney. Over the last ten years, Daniel has dedicated much of his time to poetry. He has had his own work published in his native Romania as well as Australia, which is now home, and the USA.

Daniel's passion has been sharing poetry through anthologies, bilingually in English and Romanian, as a principal translator and editor of volumes such as *Testament – 400 Years of Romanian Poetry*, a comprehensive collection of Romanian poetry in English from its origins until today. This volume won the Antoaneta Ralian Prize, most important translation award for representing Romanian literature into a foreign language, awarded by the International Bookfair Gaudeamus, Bucharest, 2019.

Other such anthologies include *The Bessarabia of My Soul* – a representation in English, of poets from the Republic of Moldova (for which Daniel was awarded the Poetry Prize of the *Literature & Art* magazine in the Republic of Moldova, 2018) and *Return Ticket from Sydney to Bistrita – A Lyrical Carousel between the Antipodes*. This work brings together, bilingually, two groups of poets living and creating 17000 kilometres apart: The Judith Beveridge Poetry Class from Sydney, and Conexiuni Literare / Literary Connections Bistrita Poetry Group from Romania.

Daniel is the current president of the Australian-Romanian Academy for Culture.

Interactive Press
Brisbane

Interactive Press
an imprint of IP (Interactive Publications Pty Ltd)
Treetop Studio • 9 Kuhler Court
Carindale, Queensland, Australia 4152
ipoz.biz/ interactive-press/
ipoz.biz/ipstore

First published by IP in 2022

© 2022 Daniel Ionita (text)

All rights reserved. Without limiting the rights under copyright reserved above, no part of this publication may be reproduced, stored in or introduced into a retrieval system, or transmitted, in any form or by any means (electronic, mechanical, photocopying, recording or otherwise), without the prior written permission of the copyright owner and the publisher of this book.

Printed in 12 pt Adobe Caslon on 14 pt Avenir Book

ISBN 9781922332820 (PB); ISBN 9781922332837 (eBook)

A catalogue record for this book is available from the National Library of Australia

Pentimento

Daniel Ionita

Interactive Press
Brisbane

Photo credit: Etienne Reynaud

Other Poetic Works by Daniel Ionita

Testament – Anthology of Modern Romanian Verse, bilingual version (English/Romanian) Minerva Publishing, 2012, 2015, with the support of Eva Foster, Daniel Reynaud & Rochelle Bews. American edition, Australian-Romanian Academy Publishing, 2017

Hanging Between the Stars, bilingual (English/Romanian) Minerva Publishing, 2013

ContraDiction, bilingual (Romanian/English) PIM Publishing, 2016

Insula Cuvintelor de Acasă (*An Island of Words from Home*, in Romanian) Limes Publishing House – Cluj Napoca, 2017

The Bessarabia of My Soul (poems from the Republic of Moldova – Daniel Ionita & Maria Tonu, MediaTon, 2018

Included in *All These Presences* (Puncher & Wattmann, 2016) and *On first looking* (Puncher & Wattmann, 2018), and *This Gift, This Poem* (Puncher & Wattmann, 2021) anthologies

Testament – 400 Years of Romanian Poetry – Daniel Ionita with Daniel Reynaud, Adriana Paul & Eva Foster (Minerva Publishing, 2019) – a bilingual representation of Romanian poetry from 1650 to the present.

Romanian Poetry from its Origins to the Present, Daniel Ionita with Daniel Reynaud, Adriana Paul & Eva Foster, Australian-Romanian Academy Publishing, 2020

Return Ticket from Sydney to Bistrita – A Lyrical Carousel between the Antipodes, Daniel Ionita, Adriana Paul, Dorel Cosma, Zorin Diaconescu, Menut Maximinian, Australian-Romanian Academy Publishing, 2021

Short Bursts of Eternity, Flying Islands, Australia, 2021

Translating the work of contemporary Romanian poets in English – over more than a decade – exerted, I believe, a deciding influence on the shape and tone of my poetry. This collection is dedicated to them.

Contents

Part 1: Faux Salvation

pig	3
I was my own dictator	4
remembering Radio Yerevan	6
my destinies	8
I am thinking of the astronauts	10
#Metoo for severed bodies	13
secret guide	14
an island of words from home	15
my letters	17
seppuku	18
concubines	19
sonnet	21
ode to Dylan Thomas	22
frustration	23
short bursts of eternity	24
pro patria	26
victim's fault	27
seven or more deadly sins – pride	28
combustion	29
detective inspector	30
cannibals	32
frozen fears	34
nutritional elements	35
lewd romance	36
punching Satan	37
consequences	40
by chance	41
regrets	43
Brian taught me everything	44

Part 2: Words for You
  instructions   47
  calling a spade, a spade   48
  Mona Lisa   50
  no water shortage this year   51
  hanging between the stars   52
  winter tears   53
  hospital emergency   54
  an intergalactic crime   55
  flighty calligraphy   56
  romance on my dirty mind   57
  creeping ahead on the zeros   59
  the coffee cup   60
  contraDiction   62
  you know love   63
  just a charade?   64
  a passing moment   65
  the subconscious of a sailboat   66
  snowing   67
  pentimento   68
  seasons   70

Part 3: Swords of the Spirit
  God, the poet   73
  the earth is the Lord's   75
  walking on a crystal leaf   77
  if I were alone in the universe   78
  this cup   80
  trivia   82
  your voice in the desert   84
  tomb reflections   85
  betrayed   86
  angel with dewdrops   87
  let's slay Santa tonight   88
  ashes of my stars   89
  abide with us   90

Part 1

Faux Salvation

*"I saved the world. Yes, me.
It was right on the edge
of its festering demise.
as I saved it with the fat hedgehog."
– Remembering Radio Yerevan*

pig

I was a pig once

no imagining,
no dreaming,
no pretence –
just simple, unostentatious piggery

I rummaged once
long ago
through your front yard
backyard too
when you turned the other way
turned the other cheek
or
turned yourself on
as the good book says

> *Strike him*
> they shouted
> *Strike him down*
> *and stick a knife, better two knives*
> *in his neck*
> *never mind him*
> *he rummages all day*
>   *all night*
>   *all the time*
>   *that's all he ever does.*

Pig! Bloody pig!

I was my own dictator

The good people from HR tell me
that I am my own boss,
the captain of my destiny.
"The sky is the limit of what you can achieve here,"
they say. I must be my own dictator.
I am Hitler and Stalin.
And if I wake up in a good mood
I am Ceaușescu.

I order my own executions,
I sign and stamp my banishment
to a faraway gulag,
> I starve to death. Nothing works:
> The following day I find myself again
> in front of the bloody computer.
> Once a month, people from HR
> disturb this ground hog day.
> They debrief me about "how
> I am adjusting to the new ecosystem…
> of the organization."
> "Good," I murmur.
> In truth, I *am* getting used to this.

I am dancing in grandiose parades,
carefully choreographed in my honour
and I clap now and then,
looking bored stiff
at my contortions,
which are worthy of a Chinese circus.
I drink children's blood
mostly my own,

and late at night
holding a gun, I order myself to sleep
for a nightmare or two.
At first light, I grab my hair
And scream to wake up.

My last HR review did not go well.

> Two minutes ago,
> Someone from "Employee Wellbeing"
> sporting a self-loathing haircut
> and two rings in his bottom lip,
> turned up in my office,
> with a security-guard.
> The hulk hands me a box, gestures
> with urgency, for me to throw all
> my items in it and buzz off.
> "But why?" I manage to whisper.
> "Because," the hair-cut bellows,
> "you do not reflect the values
> of our company.
> We have one inclusive, equitable, and diverse
> dictatorship here. No space for outliers.

remembering Radio Yerevan

Radio Yerevan tells us that we can save the world
– you, me and everybody
sitting bare-arsed on a hedgehog:
you either shave the hedgehog before sitting,
substitute someone else's arse.
or follow a directive of the Party.

So I saved the world. Yes, me.
It wasn't easy
as humanity dragged us to buggery,
right on the edge of our
festering demise.

I pricked its arse clear of muck,
two minutes before cosmic midnight
with a fat hedgehog.
Imagine that!

This was not salvation *sensu stricto*.
I am not God.
I don't love the world THAT much,

just got it out if its bother,
its pressing messiness.
A momentary delay.
No one noticed anything.

Except the hedgehog.

In the morning Radio Yerevan announces
that all remaining hedgehogs – of all things!
must report to the Red Army Choir.

My wife scolds me:
Why do you keep doing this?
Why all this thankless effort?
You've tried so many times
and you just screw it up!
You are so naïve
to believe this planet can be saved
by you and a hedgehog!
Leave them the fuck alone.
The world and that poor hedgehog…
He'll be happier singing in the Red Army Choir
And you only have a tin ear.
Yeah, yeah, I say.
Yeah, yeah, she says.

my destinies

In my first destiny, Lorelei,
I sold happiness to tourists,
as if it was fairy floss at a country fair
– they would open their mouths,
take one bite and then
throw it into the rubbish bin.

Later I would transform

into a chubby Father Christmas
– rushing around with a fed-up attitude –
dispersing toys Made in China
to those impertinent twerps.
Now and then I pulled horrid faces
when their parents were looking away.
They'd scream
"Father Christmas scared us!"
but their parents would explain,
that, in fact,
Father Christmas does not exist!

Sometimes I woke up as a customs officer
for thoughts and dreams, charging duty
for categories of high-volume personal items,
from prayers to palaver,
which lapse through people's heads –
mine, yours, everybody's.
I stacked them in a folder
for the Last Judgment.

With the passing of time,
I started introducing myself as a
professor of calligraphy, in a
screen-happy world where no one
used pens anymore.
They would just pound on keyboards
monotonous and deadly keyboards.

In a bizarre destiny
I emerged as a nocturnal clown
compelled by your voice
to gain work experience
into the amusement of your body.
Of course, Lorelei, like every other idiot
before me,
I careened into the rocks and died.
My demise was blissful
and I'd do it all again in a heartbeat.

I am thinking of the astronauts

"I am thinking of astronauts
who've beheld the image of The Whole,"
declaimed the Design & Tech teacher
teleported from some other history –
tumbling against his will.
He suffered a fall that ruptured his ankle
and dislodged a few socialist ideals from
his alcohol-happy neurons.

He was comforted by bread dipped in brandy.
Bread and plum brandy he had in abundance,
as he continued his ethereal recital,
with his mouth full and with
his eyes transfixed on the dirty-white ceiling.
We students listened to him, amazed.
We had joined him on this excursion
To the Putna Monastery[1], in Moldova,
girls and boys,
cramped in the bunk beds of
the gritty orphanage,
serving as our holiday quarters.

*

We listened fascinated to this declamation
of Shakespearian proportions,
sacred in some parts, lewd in others,
voiced in a hangover of sorts,
punctuated by joy and belligerence.

---
[1] *Putna Monastery – built and dedicated in the XVX century on the order of Stephen the Great – Prince of Moldova – situated in the province of Bukovina, in today's Romania.*

It sounded authentic and convincing –
but this could have just been the alcohol:
"The Putna Monastery," he continued,
"is now whiter than this ceiling, but it was set
on fire by the enemy, back in the old days
and skinned of all its idols."
"This monastery," he continued, "reminds me of
some sombre and messy times,
more confusing, perhaps, than those we live today –
rough times, indeed, but
far more beautiful and dignified.

"In those days Stephen the Great fought against
an implacable and atrocious enemy,
seduced noblemen's daughters,
committed countless beheadings, and ordered
the building and dedication of monasteries,
such as this one.

"Stephen atoned for his many sins
plus the GST accumulated
throughout the centuries –
since Moldova did not belong to his fathers, nor to him –
but to his children and his children's children –
as the old scribes recorded it.[2]
But, of course, he achieved a lot more, as
is the wont of history – which runs away from its unwitting
characters like diarrhea from the body of some
food-poisoned nincompoop student on a school trip.
And, yet, good ol' Stephen opened
the gate for us, so that we could enter
our creepy and sordid paradise."

---

[2] *from* The Setting Sun *by Barbu Ștefănescu Delavrancea, a play set in the last days of Stephen the Great, Prince of Moldova.*

He went quiet, as if spent, defeated,
yet still staring at the ceiling.
The sudden silence pounded my head
and I asked myself:

*Did those astronauts really see the monastery?
As they glimpsed The Whole?
And, if they did, could they also hear this soliloquy
concocted with plum brandy and bread?*

*What does it mean to be a Design & Tech teacher?
To have just enough money for bread and brandy,
and to meditate on the fate of astronauts?*

#Metoo for severed bodies

Oh my God, what's the matter with so many virus experts?
I'd request them to be shortened by the skin of their false teeth.

For the virused, on the highways, were detestably deleted
with the filthy naked figure of their bodies cut beneath.

If my leering eyes would wonder, I could visualise those breasts
for their cadaver looks stunning and doesn't even bleed.

But the multitudes will question: WTF, am I a pervert?
were the media to examine my opinion or my deed?

Melody, unzip my jodhpurs – ring those bells to circumcision
though I might be sent to prison like delinquents who offend.

I, like them, excrete discreetly, but with uttermost derision,
on "community's high standards" and the values they pretend.

I seek foolishly a hashtag, the #MeToo for severed bodies…
I find none, and that's annoying, for I always hear the ref,

or an expert on the matter – any cretin who embodies
some authority – to holler instructions till you are deaf.

secret guide

On your soul like a river, floats a world in confusion,
scrooge-like hoarding all joy – painful memories to stem
from your princes and jesters, and pursue this illusion
to be rescued from them,
to be taken to them.

Death is holding your arm; he has jumped in your bag,
just pretence, nothing true, for he's guiding the plot –
and you're ebbing and blind, death is raising his flag –
you ignore him or not,
he ignores you or not.

From your hospital bed, you are happy to borrow
one more surrogate day, phoney dawn, paper shred –
death will kiss you like Judas, nail your cross to your sorrow,
he is kissing you dead,
simple, pious, and dead.

Memories smother your dream – in your nightmare you cry –
your demise is at hand, to be cut from your stem –
yet you fly to the peak, and you spike to the sky
to be hiding from them,
to be taken to them.

an island of words from home

I left home a long time ago,
when my fragile memories
crumbled easily,
slithering away into the sand of time.
I grew and multiplied, filled out the earth,
somewhere beyond the seven seas
and at the very edge of the seventy tribes.

The memory of home dissipated – a plume of smoke
chased away by the playful wind of May –
and then, like Noah's pigeon
it flew away and never returned.

After a very long time,
from the middle of those seven seas
and from the edge of those seventy tribes,
it started to grow and raise up an island –
small at first – so I paid no attention to it.

But then, late at night,
when my wife and children were asleep,
as if in a recurring dream, I began hearing
from its direction,
a heartrending murmur:
everyday words, yet in that moment they seemed
strange to me, almost forgotten –
mother, father, love, pain, longing.

"What is this?" I asked.
"How come this island grew
right here, all-of-a-sudden,

with the seven seas and the seventy tribes and whatnot?"
"It has been here…" a voice replied.
"…ever since you arrived. It's not your fault.
It's just nature's law:
everybody who leaves their childhood home discovers
this island of words
sooner or later.
For you, today."

my letters

I sent you hundreds of letters, all open –
so that they could be read
or so I wished –
by the driver who empties the post-box,
or by the bespectacled woman who does the sorting,
and, who knows…
even by the poor postman
who pushes your correspondence, hurriedly,
through the slit of your letter box.
Maybe one of these days,
when he's not so busy, when he's bored,
he might read one of those letters.
Then he might not rush home, fight with his cheating partner,
cook some dinner, drink a beer, and watch Netflix.
Maybe he would gaze, for a moment,
towards your window, imagining who might live there.
But perhaps he might just lose concentration, crash his
yellow scooter over the barrier at the end of your street
and end up in hospital. Or dead.

seppuku[3]

I feel at home everywhere, Kamisory, my love,
and I am a stranger in all places.

I ache in the knowledge that I must come from
somewhere and from somewhere else.

This tune, this harrowing song
wells from deep within my confusion.
Squishes my heart. Pounds my brain
in staccato beats –
an excruciating potato mash.
Though seppuku remains.

If you wish to help me escape
this macabre mess,
please lead me to rest:
decapitate me in one swipe.
Be my beautiful kaishakunin.[4]
True love. This is it.

---

[3] *often called "hara-kiri" in the West, "seppuku" – stabbing oneself in the belly – is a ritual suicide that originated with Japan's ancient samurai warrior class.*
[4] *a person, usually a friend or relative, appointed to behead an individual who has performed seppuku, to swiftly end the agony.*

concubines

Your mouth was designed with a shovel,
so stop gawking at the forbidden entry

and stop shaking that pepper grinder,
for your sins are many. I,
on the other hand,

clung to mastery like an electric eel to water,
with the profligate knowledge of debaucheries

in which several desperate people
screamed all sorts of things, such as

ommanepadmehum or
praisethelord or
allahuakbar or
shabbatshalom or
thereisnogodbutme,

sycophants craving for obsession,
lusting for one or another, and hating themselves,
while drinking martinis
with their eyeballs bopping in the cocktail glass.

The only words I could muster were Yes! More!
and Oh My God!

At the precise time when your omniscience
predetermined my apotheosis
I interrupted, for some reason, my collaboration
with the forces of this unseemly,
bizarre, and pointless "democracy".

At the end of the day, when all is done
on the stroke of midnight, let's face it,
this is indeed a blatant,
squalid, and putrefied dictatorship.

And stop shaking that pepper grinder
into my martini glass –
my eyeballs are floating in it… or my balls –
either way you are welcome to have a sip.

This Louis Vuitton outfit suits you well;
including the two or three grandiose breasts
that will sink battleships with a flurry.
Therefore, I continue to cherish
your shadow, and in your name

I thrive by squashing small wild
and domestic animals.

Therefore, I have identified
you who read this poem
as: my concubines.

Bless me father, for I have sinned.

sonnet

Like lilies on a grave, a dream in tears,
canary songs for weddings or for wakes;
dull waters fill my swamps and swamp my lakes,
if hope may die, then so will all my fears.

But with a breath, or with a blink perhaps,
life makes me quiver, seizes me anew –
as all its mayhem marches into view;
while peace has fled, eluding all my traps.

For though I yearn for quiet and reserve,
tumultuous, the craze of life survives;
death looks forlorn, a little worse for wear.

I trudge through midday haze and midnight verve
and wait for life, which carelessly arrives
to push me for another day, another year.

ode to Dylan Thomas

With fierce intent and purpose will I rage –
and Death won't find me brewing cups of tea –
against that night, against old bloody age
my middle finger's up – not bent, my knee.

I shall be far from home – he'll have to run.
He'll find me in some wanton sleazy place
with dancing and with drinking and the fun
of fulsome wenches riding on my face.

And while Death grabs me, I will sip champagne.
One final "petite mort"? – oh sure! I would!
For life was good! – with all its fucking pain –
I'd bloody push the rewind button if I could.

frustration

One side of the coin dies
in pain
because it
cannot see the other.
It knows full well that
it does not even
stand the indecent chance
of teenage schoolboys, who
push each other out of the way
to peep through a keyhole
into the girls' dressing room.
That is why, for thousands of years,
ever since coins have been unearthed
archaeologists, when they find them,
all report the same thing:
"Today a coin was discovered, displaying
the eternal pain of frustration."

short bursts of eternity

That knife… that knife is twisting
between my ribs, scratching the bone.
You wonder why I remain silent?
The pain is so great that I could not
even make a sound…
My gnarled face
remains transfixed – imagine it
like a framed photograph –
a still from some black & white horror film.

My bones are being crushed,
patiently, methodically,
starting with the toes and fingers,
then ankles and wrists,
as if according to a protocol –
equally gruesome and meticulous.

The next horror pushes me out
into the path of pain,
like the shovel throwing dirt
in front of a bulldozer.

Are you still here?

My belly is sliced open.
In the horrid moments
when I can lift my head I
see my innards:
liver, stomach, lungs,
intestines being dragged out,
I'd be wearing my heart… I swear…
if I had a sleeve, that is.

I can just make out some sharp tongs
about to pull out my eyeballs.
For minuscule slices of time I
manage to find a place,
a small corner inside myself, where I
can exist, away from from this pain.

Count a few milliseconds. Can you?
This is the time I
am bereft of feeling anything – and I
hide there for an extremely brief eternity,
hoping to reach the next one.
Yet, incessant pain rages and
shreds are torn from me,
vicious tears.

I know you cannot imagine this. How could you?
It is too grotesque, too bizarre to fathom,
unless you've been crushed yourself.
I curl inside there –
in the eye of the storm –
in that small space, that tiny edge, that point
without light, words, thoughts…
Suddenly pain and death look shabby,
cheap, remote, invisible, and mute.
Although dread still rages, death still bites –
but now this happens somewhere outside.
Very outside now. Very somewhere else.
I find myself inside a Sabbath of sorts.

I am being spared, for now –
this pain is stringently divided
between short bursts of eternity.

pro patria

I have died once or twice before,
for the motherland and the nation.
Or so I thought, giving up my ghost
plundered away by youthful imbecility –
displayed with the flourish –
of blunderhead anorexic saints,
painted willy-nilly inside worship houses,
inane and full of creepy piety – like was I.

But I've had enough! Therefore, you
can go on being offended,
exuding your ideological excrement,
pooping a collective indigestion,
instantaneous, putrid and exploding
across the galaxy, only to be sucked
into a black hole parallel with the sinkhole.

I've had enough hearing about your abject patriotism!
You flare-up at nothing,
with your beloved motherland egressing from your arse
like a knotted-up flatulence.
You artificially inseminated bovines!

victim's fault

When I said that I am a vegetarian and
do not consume dead animals,
I did not mean that I wouldn't tear
a bite out of your body.
Maybe on a full moon,
my need for human flesh awakens,
rises up from its lair, stretches for a bit,
then lurches on the prowl.
You could have stayed at home,
of course, watched some
TV series, or read a book,
maybe make love to someone,
to yourself, whatever.
What now?
Teeth sinking into soft flesh.
Blood flowing freely.
Gluttony.
See what you've done?
All. Your. Fault.

seven or more deadly sins – pride

Some people think they know everything.
They don't, but I do.
Some people feel they can do anything.
They cannot, but I can.
Some kiss the dust tread upon by the Grand Fat Burrito
and believe that humility will save them.
And good on them! But I don't.
For the meek may well inherit the earth and yet –
they have no idea of what they'll do with it,
dancing to the tune of "dust to
dust, and ashes to ashes."
Beware of pride, they tell me, it walks before the fall.
Ah, sure it does… But it marches on, does not sneak by.
Not like you! You, fruitage of a marmoset's bottom!
Tell me: would anyone else say this to your face?
Let me be clear: a speck of dandruff of my head
is worth one hundred ideas
of genius from yours.

combustion

My chromosomes abound with wasteful flair
it's such a pity that the earth is flat...
If it was square, or conical at that
I could have dozed away in my electric chair.

Those termites that keep squirming in my brain
dancing at sunset and at dawn
I see how crisply they crawl over my eyeballs,
while I, a coward, wallow like a swain.

Reflecting on this grim and grotty scene
I'm comforted by terrors through the night
I crave to puff myself, to glitter bright
But, in the end, I swallow this tedious routine.

I think therefore I am, Monsieur… and doing what I must
to princes of this bog, whom I abhor.
They all declare for peace, while they prepare for war…
and I shall freeze them – ready to combust.

detective inspector

The old man, naked and dead, was wearing a mask.
And a condom, as required by lockdown rules.
The girl, of stellar intensity,
was also wearing a mask. Just the mask for her.
Essential worker she was, as stipulated in the regulations.
Apparently, she was so hot that the pervert started to burn –
his screams of delight,
plunged into a terrified and desperate wailing.
He slowly realised he would die and curled up into a foetal
position.
Just before losing consciousness, with his last whisper
he called the masked girl "mommy".
He tried to reach for one last supreme suckle
at her smallish left boob, but perished – with the despair
of those who die of thirst, or burning at the stake –
imprinted on the remains of his charred face.

When the police arrived, the detective
interrogated the girl, recording all of this
in his report. He would await the lab's analysis,
again, as per the regulations.

The girl, still naked, still with her mask immaculately on,
confirmed the old guy wore both his mask and
the condom, as they began to consummate this
grisly coitus interruptus.
They could not find the latter,
suspecting heat disintegration,
along with the member it was rolled on.
Still, the detective was positive
that forensic analysis would prove it,

and this is how he ended his report:
"...Therefore, I expect to declare the inexistence
of any suspicious circumstances, be they
standard or unusual, and furthermore, I recommend
no need for any further criminal investigation."

"This is so boring," muttered the detective to himself.
"I want a real case of murder, with cruelty, maybe
torture, eyes gouged out, testicles ripped off, members severed.
People envy the detective's job, but they have
no idea how boring this gig really is. Naked girls,
dead old losers, it's about as exciting as it gets."

cannibals

Remember the mini cannibals?
You always told me to stay calm,
when those tiny flesh gobblers were
hacking chunks from my body,
as large as continents!
I was already missing a third of my bones,
one eye and half of the left ear.
I was kicking at them with the one
leg still hanging from my hip and with my fists.
They would shriek, startled,
draw back for a second,
but then hurtle forward – dumb hate
burning in their devilish eyes,
and sparkling on their bloody teeth.
Two of them hacked into my ribs,
as five or six kicked and bit each other
over part of my liver.

*Why did you sit, indifferent and
with a somewhat amused look on your face,
at the little round table on the terrace,
telling me to remain calm –
while biting from an apple and
speaking with your mouth full?*

One of the wretched things managed to get behind me,
Stuck his finger through the left earhole inside my brain,
drew it out scraping some grey matter
with his tongue from underneath his fingernail.
Suddenly the bedlam was pierced
by his mini-cannibalistic scream,

his eyes rolled over and he dropped dead.
The other mini cannibals looked at each
other in fright, ran away,
disappearing in a puff of dust
down one of the roads which lead to Rome.

Please explain, what is your bloody point?
Why just shrug your shoulders and look at me
with that superior smile, as if to say:
I told you so!?

frozen fears

I fear this black-iced road
leading inward
I fear all this snowstorm
ravaging
the permafrost of my thoughts.
I fear the North, the South, the East, the West
together with all other extremities
where I lost most things
including the last of my virginities
somewhere in that frigid wasteland.
I fear the unthawed blues of
Mondays and Wednesdays
I fear the snowy boots stomping on my coffin
I fear the glacial flowers sprouting on my eyeballs
and I fear, too, both of my indigo hands
and my cryogenic heart – shifty floes sliding on
the tainted sediments of my unmelted memory.

nutritional elements

The consciousness proposed by Descartes
cogito ergo sum and all that jazz –
is this an argument for a superior
form of existence?
What about the (implicit?) opinion of
colonies of bacteria and viruses,
which asserted, in front of the
United Nations Commission for Micro-Organisms Rights
that I should embody a farm
for growing their nutritional needs?

And that my family, friends, foes, foetuses
work, holidays, love, hate, beautiful and
despicable experiences,
arts and sciences – all of these –
are nothing more, save for simple strategies
meant to keep me preoccupied,
unconscious of the fact that I am being
consumed.
Like in the movies.

lewd romance

A mighty gladiator of this life,
I carry through the dark a wilted wreath –
like muddy kisses, hanging in the evening,
sewn by cruel demons, in hell beneath,
to deeply smear my thoughts, which long ago,
bore bitter struggles pushed by velvet rage –
making me suckle at some flaccid bosoms –
and pay for sleazy dreams a handsome wage,
while wooing lazily, in sordid fashion,
composted wenches resting on a bed,
who carried on their bellies abject symbols
and breathed a putrid odour as they bled –
bones quashed and scuttled in a glass, asunder,
I slurped their boil, devious and vile
coarse rummagings through hangovers of bodies
tailored from cursing and from abject bile.

But then, already rusty from my weeping
while sacrificing to this holy storm,
I'd jump in terror from my restless sleeping
and smitten, I would desecrate your form –
for it was you injecting all this creeping
abiding terror, as my nightly norm.

Today, in stoic solitude and gloom
I lay beneath my linden tree to rest,
to sing old tales of bravery and doom,
and play some lewd romances full of zest,
of men who fight for life's illusive plume
and for a handsome woman's ample breast.

punching Satan

We are sitting at a big table in a swish restaurant.
Beeeeeeeeg table, satin tablecloth.
Is this a fine dining yum cha, if there is such a thing,
or a proper formal French setting?
I cannot tell.
It is old fashioned,
yet stylish rather than quaint,
classy and subtle, rather than overdrawn.
Vaulted ceilings, Corinthian columns,
you've seen the movie; you know the style.
My family is here, around the table.
I am part of a rather large tribe.
Now, if you press me,
I cannot tell you precisely
where everyone is seated.
Dreams are like that: a veracity of sorts is assumed,
even if important information
is missing.

(Of course, I could name each one –
wife, children, sons-in-law, grandchildren, parents –
but this would all be post-dream,
therefore, post-factum.
Trust me on this – they are all there:
an incontrovertible fact in this dream.)

Now... right to my left, sits Satan –
the only one I know where to place, with confidence.
Nice looking guy, tall, dark, and handsome,
perhaps in his mid-thirties, charcoal
or black formal suit –

shiny glitter through the fabric –
I'm sure it is an Armani or Hugo Boss,
not Brioni or Tom Ford.
Can't he afford the later? Is Satan thrifty?
White shirt, blood-red satin tie,
made of the same material
as the tablecloth. Maybe he is stingy.
Interesting. Or maybe this is just a distraction.
Wait! It is a bow tie.
No, it is a traditional tie.
It is both a bow tie and... never mind.
Now, a couple of questions occur to me...
Do they occur to you?

The first: *How do I know he is The Evil One?*
I just know. One hundred percent sure.
Question two, once I get over
this first terrifying realisation:
What the hell... is he doing here?
Is he part of the family? God forbid!!
No. I don't think so.
Gosh... at least I hope not!
He makes conversation – relaxed, unassuming,
Canadian accent (I am a translator and I know my accents.
Why Canadian? God only knows –
He invented the Devil after all –
either way, he sounds freakishly mellow...)
He talks about the menu, and then shifts
to the galloping price of property in Sydney
(Lucifer would do that, it makes perfect sense.
If anyone talks to you about Sydney house prices,
they ARE Satan, or at least sent by Satan).
Another fact I am sure of –
I know WHY he is here:
he wants to hurt one of those I love.
Who? I cannot tell. Someone.

Under the satin folds of the tablecloth,
I make my right hand into a tightly clenched fist.
I wait for an opportune moment,
pretending I'm interested in his chatter,
waiting until he's mid-sentence...
then I strike him fast and hard,
right on his nose! As you do.
Muhammad Ali
would be proud of such a strike.
Or maybe Mike Tyson. Indeed, Mike Tyson.

I know, dreams... are dreams –
we cannot control the narrative.
The moment I threw the punch, I woke up.
I wish I could tell you that he ended up in hospital.
Or in hell. Same thing – both start with h
and are horrible places by all accounts.

But while sipping my coffee that morning,
I asked myself why did my dream story
not follow that of Job or Jacob,
and their sparring with God.
Am I not good enough?

consequences[5]

My darling, I said I'm not stirred by conclusions,
I couldn't care less about them, don't you see?
And all your assumptions are only delusions.
It's just consequences that are bothering me.

We gaze at each other in a morbid chagrin
and make love tormented, with a passion of sorts,
while time, unforgiving, is judging our sin –
the truth, above all, overshadowed by words.

I pretend a lot, for I feign to deceive,
and people believe me, though it's plainly absurd –
but then, like a lamb, immature and naïve,
I give up my horns and return to the herd.

But let us be clear, there's no room for confusion,
for no one supposes that love comes for free!
And I am indifferent to assumptions, conclusions…
It's just consequences that bother me.

---

[5] *Inspired by a song of Valeriu Sterian.*

by chance

My aunt Rodica's cat
never catches a single mouse
because
by chance
those mice are much more clever
than his excellency Tutuluț the Taupe tomcat.

Being well-fed by Aunt Rodica,
he prefers small morsels of cat food,
which appear, as if by magic,
day after day, in his little saucer
by the entrance door –
instead of bothersome mice, who are
neurotic, whimsical, downright recalcitrant,
with no fixed address.

Also, by chance,
my piano teacher,
Miss Iliescu,
is still a virgin at seventy-nine
and proclaims this
as others might boast about receiving the Nobel Prize.
She used to teach piano
to the children of a Mavrocordat lady,
a progeny from an obscure branch
of a famous Phanariot family in Bucharest.

Sometime, somewhere, during all that,
seemingly by chance,
I even reach adolescence,
but this occurs before I am born,

and then born again, by sheer chance
a few years following these events,
a consequence of a mystical encounter,
involving all my probable parents in culpable fashion.
Or at least this is the current gossip –
if you are to believe all
that people blather about.

regrets

All the world's regrets advance towards me –
press, crush, stifle, and throttle me
push me towards an abyss
destined for my fall.
I try to arrest this by grabbing
big shreds of anguish and remorse –
anything that might be flying by –
about lovers, children, or grandparents –
unfinished dreams, be they dry or wet.

I wished to explain to you
that I regretted everything
one could feel heartbreak for –
but I keep stumbling
upon candles for the dead
and all the paraphernalia
besetting your bloody, yet inconsequential
wake and funeral.
I have no more sorrows left.
This is somewhat perplexing and disappointing
and I regret even opening this subject.

Brian taught me everything

to Brian, naturally

before I even went to school
Brian already taught me everything
to ride a bike and swim across the pool
yes, Brian taught me everything

and when I met the first cute girl
Brian – oh man! – he knew a thing or two
how to hold her hand and how to make her twirl
he taught me what to do

eventually I went to war
was it in summer, or in spring?
He taught me how to aim and shoot
for Brian surely knew that kind of thing

one lucky day I found a wife
as Brian taught me not to do,
and settled for a crazy life,
while Brian didn't have a clue.

These days I'm old and grey and watch the sky
as Brian showed me how – so many years ago
remembering all the good old days, gone by
when Brian taught me all there is to know.

Part 2

Words for you

*"I'll write a poem – you'll be my muse –
Perhaps its verses will be torn and confuse,
For even Shakespeare can't fix it, you see…
It doesn't matter – to be or not to be."*
– Dinu Olăraşu

instructions

I will be home, or maybe not, when you arrive.
The soup is in the empty fridge; just warm it up.
The ghost of lettuce and the shadow of a buttercup –
I'm sure there's something, maybe nothing, to contrive.

You can't do anything about the cough, should it persist:
Watch some TV, there is nothing on, unless there is
Or better, read a book with missing pages – hers or his,
And settle in the guest room, should it still exist.

calling a spade, a spade

I dream I just turned seventeen
the day I go to the village shop and kindly ask
the woman behind the counter
to please give me a vase. No response.
The price tag says fifty dollars. Is it too much?
I ask her again. She seems distracted.
Pulls a spade from the corner.
I never knew she had one tucked there
or I did, to be honest,
but avoided looking at it –
corner-of-the-eye kind of ignorance.
"What am I going to do with this spade, miss?"
"You will need one, young man."
Her words flow like snowflakes,
melting from her lips.
"Today, or tomorrow, or in fifty years from now,
but you will definitely need it.
One day, if you do
something worthwhile with your life,
you will have enemies.
What will you bury them with?"
I ask her to marry me.
"No", she replies.
"Why not?" I say. "You look like the marrying type,"
(you could say such things in those days)
"I already have a husband," she says.
This confuses me a little bit:
"I feel you could handle another one quite well,"
I mumble.

"FIFTY DOLLARS! And get out!" she barks.
But then she acts contrite:
"This is all the advice I can give you for your money."

"Worth every penny!" I reply.
"This is a LOT more
than I expected!"
She throws the spade at me.
I feel all of Edvard's scream swelling inside of me.
The sweet rays of the dawn
are already dripping down my face,
filled with the excitement of marital bliss!

Mona Lisa

Just give me your hand, Mona Lisa, and flee,
leave mouldy museums to quibble and moan –
the world waits outside, made of flesh and of bone,
with rain and with sunshine, with mountains and sea.

For hundreds of years you have hung on this wall,
in hope Leonardo will somehow appear –
while loafers and fools gave you praises or smear
and packed like sardines, they remained in your thrall.

Your gaze speaks a playful or insolent tale –
as thousands of critics are wont to explain –
but what matter words, be they wise or mundane,
when up on this wall hangs your heart, by a nail?

I'll wait till the evening at the pub down the lane
that is crowded with people made of flesh and of bone,
leave stuffy old Louvres to quibble and moan
and we'll dance in the sunshine and run in the rain.

no water shortage this year

I was lost in a winter, long ago,
during a windless snowfall.
I started melting, weeping with joy –
trickling
down the left breast
of this girl who felt like getting out into the yard
to dance naked,
in the idle rhythm of the first snow.
Once arrested into this dance with her, that was the end.
Thousands of us perished that day –
a flake genocide of sorts.
I was already no more than a tepid drop
when the girl returned to the kitchen.
She switched on the tap
whispering absentmindedly
"There won't be a water shortage this year…"

hanging between the stars

My heart was left hanging between some stars
my hope snowing lonely
towards the surface of the earth.
You were beside me but I saw you less and less.
Why did I follow you up there?
Why did you leave without me?
Questions ephemeral as a snowstorm.
I didn't dare ask you where we were going,
nor why the path was no longer visible.
The morning caught me singing sad carols,
which quickly froze,
pinned over the abyss.

Now I don't feel your presence anymore.
You left my heart hanging between the stars.
Between snowflakes you wave to me
and call for me to wait.

winter tears

Why did you disrobe those winter winds
bestowed upon you by the Almighty when
He expelled you from my Garden?
You were more beautiful than
the fire-sword angels, more dazzling
than the mini-skirted girl in the photograph
which I dug out when I smashed your tombstone.

Are you cold?
I will kill that goat, slash its throat,
to fashion you a jacket from its hide.
It will accept its fate with serenity
in harmony with this rainy winter afternoon.
It will kneel and slowly close its eyelids,
like the fall of a rusty leaf
in this windless and overcast plain.

*

I lay the jacket on your shoulders –
fragrant like freshly picked apples –
and over those sugar-berry breasts.
Your eyes well up.
You turn your face slightly
to wipe them off
with your little finger,
while you feign arranging your hair.
Cold raindrops are now falling and
they mix with the warm tears on your cheek.
Winter is weeping with you.

hospital emergency

I did call for the ambulance – was feeling queasy.
Fuck! Those asses dropped me at a brothel, packed
full of whores. The dumb twits cannot read
a simple instruction...
What did I expect?! Not prostitutes, that's for sure
and certainly not dressed up as nurses and doctors.
I asked the receptionist:
"Is this the hospital they call 'The Brothel'?"
"No," said he. "You got it wrong, mate.
This is, in fact, the brothel we call 'the Hospital'."
Boobs, boobs, boobs, and more boobs.
My condition improved, somewhat.
Even the grim reaper would be stopped in his tracks
for a moment or two
by those boobs, some of them as substantial
as the moons of Jupiter.
I pray that when I die
I should slide on the toboggan inside their canyon –
it might be into paradise or it might be into hell.
Only may this ride last an eternity or two.
Amen.

an intergalactic crime

You fly, silent comet, through an endless expanse,
and the clouds of my galaxy chime like a psalm.
An angel is hiding, awaiting his chance,
beholding you tender and calm.

Your hair is of stardust entwined with dark matter,
which flows on your shoulders in heavenly flares.
And touched by a strand, on his forehead, aflutter,
the angel is smiling. He cares...

Your eyes, velvet moon sparks, pierce him –
my soul is a nightmare, with brimstone aglow...
A Holy One? Angel? Once you've gone, so you know,
I'll grab him and throttle him slow.

flighty calligraphy

My words stick to you.
They bind like a calligraphic tattoo,
thousands of years old, as if chiselled by
a Chinese scribe from the Emperor's palace,
lovesick, craving for his sweetheart.
Meanwhile, the calligraphy
runs faster and faster, flightier, and flightier,
until I cannot decipher it.
Now and then I add a word,
which slots into an available space.
Then you place your index finger
to my lips to stop the charge of words.
"Handsome is as handsome does," you whisper.
Hmm… Can my deeds follow their own capricious path
on your body as my words?

romance on my dirty mind

I am a hopeless romantic.
I bring you flowers,
just because your smile
dispatches me to thirty-seven parallel paradises
where thirty-seven Adams and Eves lie
naked and without shame
to beat the daily tedium
beneath the shadow provided by
the Tree of Knowledge.

As I brush your hair
with the fingertips of my left hand
you read that magazine – and I chuckle to myself
seeing your glasses slide off your nose.
I smile as you push them up, again and again.

How does that story go?
The one you read to me yesterday, about
the man with three sets of multi-coloured dentures,
which exploded on the train coming home from the office?
Did it make as big a mess as they said on the news?
Did the government offer free therapy
for the commuters in that carriage, and maybe
free monochromatic dentures?

But forget about that: I cannot
help it spying with the corner of my eye,
as you casually lift the strap of your nightdress –
and I feel hurried and hoisted
by an array of exquisite thoughts.
I have eaten your forbidden fruit,

now squished in my mouth.
God knows I am a hopeless romantic
with a very dirty mind.

creeping ahead on the zeros

I'm creeping ahead on the zeros,
spending twenty lives in Cuba Street –
at the Harbor Market full of cheesy heroes,
and of topless beauties, beating down the heat.

The Bond movie was average, we agree
but the walk downhill is very nice;
all the shops are closed on Lambton Quay
and we stop to kiss, once or twice.

But I'm creeping ahead on the zeros
spending ninety lives in Cuba Street,
when that preacher – shouting "you've killed Christ!" –
gets me weeping, speechless, in my seat.

Will you hold my hand again tomorrow?
Should I drop my glasses down the hill?
What if I attempt to get them back
and can't return in time to pay the bill?

I photographed the tulips, that morning, in the Garden
near the old Sharella Motor Inn –
since then your raven hair turned gray, and yet
love, for us, has never lost its spin.

And I still creep ahead on my zeros,
wasting countless lives in Cuba Street,
just to win this bloody game of Seven Up –
but, if lose to you again, I'll think you're just as sweet.

the coffee cup

I had just completed unraveling all
that was meant for you to have unraveled,
filled with a guilt-ridden dream –
touching your lips for just a moment –
from which a myriad of confessions, penances,
and absolutions couldn't save me.

Damnation was as real as my breathing
and I kept mixing it into the coffee –
reflecting the hue of your pupils,
surrounded by the white porcelain
of the coffee cup.
It reminded me of the fairy tale
in which a silver spoon would
would mix black coffee
in a Japanese cup for
a thousand and one nights.

Time absconded and I hated
the thought that it would reappear.
Therefore, in my mind, I smash against rocks
the heads of all clockmakers in the universe.
The trite sound of the mobile phone
tortured me, and those
who kept asking how I was doing,
plunged knives into my heart.

When I finished my coffee…
the last sips slipping away
along with the dream.
I made myself another,

mixing it with a silver spoon
in the Japanese cup,
ready for the next unravelling,
for the next damnation.

contraDiction

On occasions, I see you through old windows, now rotten,
a diaphanous ghost, drifting smoky and thin,
and my memories arise between tears long forgotten,
like a love that has been,
like old loves that have been.

As you reached out to me, hells and edens shaking,
I grab at them dreading, knowing well that I'll die
but I feel you hedonic, my body aching,
and I'm longing to cry,
and I'm longing to cry.

Though I pushed you away… you remain by my side?
you're my life – yet your death might just even the score
you enslave me with memories, you submit as my bride
whom I love and abhor,
whom I love and abhor.

you know love

You know love by the leaves, the flowers,
the light and the road.
Yet
the leaves on the coffin might turn yellow,
the flowers on the grave might wilt,
the candles at the forehead of the dead
might wax out,
But
the road of the funeral procession
is never complicated.

just a charade?

My heart dries and crumbles in the sun, in the heat,
its shadow and tear lay unholy, afraid.
I am hoping for nightfall to conceal my deceit
is this a love story, or just a charade?

Death crouches ill-boding, with manners askew,
he munches on bones and spits on the ground
inquiring wryly if I know about you –
I lie as before: we are well, we are sound.

"She no longer loves you!" sneers Death in a slight.
"Be gone, stupid demon!" I shout in dismay.
But inside I am devoured by sadness and spite
and I'm burning to beat and chase him away.

"You're as dumb as a heart drying out in the heat!"
vomits Death from the tomb side – as I tremble, afraid.
Only nightfall protects me and conceals my defeat:
Is it Death? Is it Love? Or just a charade?

a passing moment

Her fate was hanging overhead like the sword of Damocles
such as it is waiting for each one of us –
and it will come to pass without fail.

She sat in my lap, a flabbergasted and frightened deer,
stunned in front of the headlights of life.
"This is just a passing moment,"
I said, trying to soothe her.

"Life itself is just a passing moment," she answered.
"A string of passing moments and fleeting situations
culminating with one –
the last –
when I die – when my being and universe fuse.

Leave your hand in mine for the moment…
In this way my time will ebb more gently."

the subconscious of a sailboat

to Petronela and Dinu (and their sailboat)

Send a zephyr my way on the indigo sea,
let us sail on the *Bosphorus* with no wave of goodbye...
No one cares if you live, no one weeps if I die.
People scorn our love, let us sail and be free.

I await like a mast: quiet, lonesome, and brave.
Take that lifesaver ring, and your skirt of chiffon
for the sailboat, so eager to rise on the wave,
wants to prove if you are here, wants to know if you're gone.

With our boat on the waves, whitecaps kissing its bow,
we will sway on the sea, be it sunshine or mist,
and I'll fashion a garland of shells for your brow,
so you know I'm alive as I prove you exist.

snowing

to Jo – in memoriam

snowing on the dead in a velvety array
snowing Sundays, weeping, lost between my Wednesdays
snowing from my soul and frosting in my eye
snowing cemeteries, longing for your birthdays

snowing on the blossom, mournful in the clay
snowing through my winter, idle to depart
snowing while you dream and snowing while I pray
snowing on the anguish bludgeoning my heart.

snowing on our love, a compromise amiss
snowing like a kiss that Judas meant for you
snowing when you're flying into the abyss
snowing on my tears with sorrow from the blue

while the snowing ended, yet the buds remain
on the frigid landscape – craggy but content –
just the flake of winter in my heart will reign
yearning for your smile and frozen in lament.

pentimento

Misty hues strangle me
startling monsters
jumping at me from the painting easel.
I still breathe your watercolor.
Love and Death – those horny monsters –
kiss me –
in this lugubrious ménage à trois.
I am licked by a rain
with insane shapes, as if by drawn by Dali.

I demure about traces of footprints
leading from the alehouse to the cemetery.
My body rushes to welcome you in,
You, indeed, who cannot ever die,
just as you cannot ever love.

I walked to meet you – my smile was stuck
with glue on my face,
my applause mechanical,
my bowing before you like a shoe-shiner.

I walked to meet you – indeed, you
for whom I paint another layer, which
centuries later will be a pentimento
revealing our tryst.

I paint over it with a poison of vanity –
my death sentence, you know: 'Pride goes before
the fall' and all that jazz.

Yet there is a reward for all this,
transient as it may be:
On my tongue I taste
the watercolour of your body.

seasons

I pray for snows to settle white and pure,
ice flowers in your window, frosty spree,
the fireplace – to muse or to demure –
I gaze at you, I smile, I sip my tea.

When, in the green of spring, we drink the dew
of early mornings, sweet and tender tryst –
and step through grass of moist and limpid hue –
our love will scatter with the buds of mist.

While later, through the summer's reddish day
with hearts and flowers open wide in sunny gleams,
the jasmine queen of night will fill our play
with tender scents and tinges for our dreams.

But lend me just an autumn, from all these,
with yellow leaves to stutter in the gale,
your eyes to linger into mine with ease,
your hand in mine, through rain along our trail.

Part 3

Swords of the spirit

*"Your sword
slashes the marrow and the sinew,
it cleaves the essence, reason and desire."
– The Book of Hebrews 4:12*

God, the poet

After I wrote the first indecent poem
I cut off my leg,
the left or the right, I cannot remember.
I would have left it alone,
but it was walking me into the tedium of daily sin
and so, I cut it off.

After I finished one hundred lascivious poems,
I gouged out my eye.
The right or the left, I forgot.
I would have left it in its place,
but it was staring only
at the incessant debauchery.
I took it out with a silver spoon,
attentively, so that I don't make a mess,
inside my perfectly sordid paradise.

After a thousand lewd poems
I was about to sever one of my hands,
the left or the right – no matter –
when a worrying thought occurred to me:
if I go on like this, I'd soon be confined to
playing only with my bacchanalian poetic ideas –
instead of with myself –
this is important to me.
(Is it to you? Maybe it's just me…)

Where were we? …After one million libidinous poems
I am, again, on my way to my abattoir du jour,
where I carry out these self-mutilations
when I see God walking on the street.

Just like that, there He is!
On the way to the markets.
He says, "I'm on my way to sell poems:
gold poems, white garments poems, and eye salve poems.
Do you want some? You will not regret them."
He sounds convincing and seems … well-versed…

So, I purchase from him a ditty,
ointment for my eye,
the one still hanging from its socket.
He manufactured it from dust
mixed with spital in His pierced hands.
(He diagnosed me as a *poetus orbi*.
"Trust me," He said. "I once worked as a family G.P.
in the Nazareth shire, district of Galilee.")

"There's hope for you, too," He goes on,
"for I produced decent poets out of all sorts
of losers, fishermen, widows, to tax-collectors,
lepers, pharisees, ordinary whores,
and even some extraordinary ones."

As He steps away on the footpath,
I understand,
for the first time,
that God cannot sin,
even though He permits into existence
a whole heap of daily poems –
most very sleazy indeed.

the earth is the Lord's

to my grandfather, Ioan Ogrean

The place I came from is a fading memory.
Now I abide in a realm with rocks and waves,
where yesterday knew not what was doomed for tomorrow,
and today is born like a fragmented brown universe,
a continent, a country, a world perhaps.
I remember how, long ago,
a child played with a punctured football
on a cobblestoned street
on the outskirts of a faraway city
near a boulevard, a park, and a drinking fountain

But for many years now,
I've been walking past gum trees
on the edge of a place where the ocean kisses
the shore, and then recedes, only to start
over again, in a foreplay of sorts.
And there I dip my toes,
thinking that maybe tomorrow
the universe will sprout anew, and God
will rush Her Second Coming to collect the rent,
and stop this nonsense of geography
and history, and politics and culture – all
invented by humans…
So many confusing and contrived entities,
in which children,
like some cheery trees in cherry orchards,
cannot imagine, say, gum trees and vice versa;
they think it's just them
who can kick around a punctured ball,
or watch the sun set into the ocean.

As for me, I am an island, or even a continent,
though one floating here and there –
with no fixed address.
Or I am a city,
perhaps a cherry tree or a eucalyptus,
a pebble on the ocean shore.

Rather, I am all at once, because
the thought of being just of one nature, belonging
to just one country, seeing just one ocean,
this weighs on me like a coffin lid
nailed above my face
and I can't breathe – I push, and push,
and I SCREAM!
Why should I suffer like this?
It might make more sense to respond
like my grandfather, when he got asked: "Why,
Mr. Ogrean,
did you leave your home country at seventy-four years of age?
You had a nice house in Bucharest, a good pension…
Why come to live in this strange city, so far from home?"
To this he always replied with a paraphrase
from a psalm of David:
"The earth is the Lord's, and the fullness thereof,
the world and all who dwell therein."[6]

---

[6] *Psalm 24:1.*

walking on a crystal leaf

I was walking on a crystal leaf
careful to avoid the edges
The sound of my steps formed into clear, cymbal
melodies, each more beautiful than the other.
The leaf, I know, will break at some point,
sending me to my death,
but my steps echo for a while,
sometimes joyful, at other times sad, yet always clear.
I hear your voice:
This sound I shall keep.
This sound I shall remember forever.
This cymbal sound will join
with the sound of the steps of many others –
some of them may be like you, others not,
but all will be in tune with the universe.
No longer will you be stepping in fear
on the dainty edge of a crystal leaf:
rather, you will walk my streets of gold
and my pavements of diamond.
Thus, your song will resound in the infinity of light,
and echo with the gladness of angels.

if I were alone in the universe

if I were alone in the universe,
like a mouse at the bottom
of an empty forty-gallon drum,
nothing else would matter.

There would be no one to care, to love, to hate,
or even to pass me by
on some intergalactic boulevard.
I would not understand my lonely tear,
for I would not have seen a mother weeping.
Even lonely old people weep sometimes,
but only because, long ago,
they have known love, requited or not.

But if I was alone in the universe,
I wouldn't know of love,
nor that love begets life, and life beckons death.
So, my tear would be nothing – if nothing could indeed exist.
It could not be lonesome, nor regretful.
This tear in the corner of my eye would be meaningless,
Yet, this makes no sense either.
For there would be no meaning in the first place,
to be devoid of, or to be lost.
Dread would not be my nightly companion,
if I were alone in the universe
and my heart would not skip a beat for anything,
for even *good* and *bad* could not wage war
in a universe where I would be the only one.
If I were alone in the universe,
nothing, including me, would matter.
But because you are here,

and because you have been here from the beginning,
I have known love and sin, and loneliness, and tears,
and good, and bad, and death, and life:
all that ever existed, all that is,
and all that will be.

this cup

I was conceived in iniquity
and in sin I was born –
so… it cannot be me,
a child of debauchery and heartache,
who should save the nations.
Therefore, my Lord
take this cup from me –
it is full with vinegar meant to be sipped
to its bitter dregs just so
that dying humanity remembers eternity –
and hand it over to the other wretched betrayed,
groaning right now in Gethsemane.
I pray lead my steps
on pleasant walkways,
clear and sunny,
leading towards my day-to-day Hell.
I am used to it.
Honestly, when this conversation started,
I was rather craving for a different cup,
one with stolen sweet waters.
But you convinced me
to swallow this terrible little book,
which was sweet like honey in my mouth,
but, in my stomach, it became wormwood,
so bitter, that I had to sell
all that hay and wood and reed –
which I was saving for a rainy day –
and buy from you at an extravagant price,
refined gold, white clothes and salve for my eyes.
And yet, despite all this,
the straight and narrow path is not entirely clear to me,

and it certainly does not offer an easy walk
through these daily unforgiving catastrophes.
Only your pierced hand reaches out to me
every now and then
to caress my forehead.

trivia

Your great terror will prevail and might even
daunt, frighten, horrify me, one day. One day.
But… in all other days
your spine-chilling threat is dimmed
by the noise of the wind,
by the clamour of the playing children,
the murmur of kissing lovers,
the jingle of pots and pans in the kitchen –
by a bamboozling assortment of the random
bedlam of everyday life:
this staccato beat, this incessant pulse of the mundane.

Your posturing and your frightful face are regularly blurred,
by the energy required for the minutia of existence,
like when I'm brewing my coffee, or chatting to a friend,
or looking into the eyes of my child.
Doesn't this annoy you? Doesn't it really piss you off?

I mean, look at you!!
So monstrous and devastating, conclusive, implacable –
you, which no one can escape, you are forgotten,
overwhelmingly neglected,
thoroughly undefined, not much more than
a fleeting, fading thought.

Stop shouting! I know: some day,
I'll surely bloody die.
I heard you, but forgive me please:
if you're not here to take me right now,
then get the fuck out of my house,
for I have more important things to do

like mixing my potato salad
with olive oil, lemon, mayonnaise, a
bit of Hot English Mustard,
spring onion and some finely cut dill.
"Death, where is your sting?
Where is your victory?"[5]

---

[5] *1 Corinthians 15:55.*

your voice in the desert
after Petre Anghel

Sir, I heard your voice in the desert
like the sound of cold water over rocks
like the whisper of shady trees
like breath, like life –
and then, that barren and parched wasteland
teemed with rivers and flowers and birds,
with goodness, with mercy, with love.
And ever since, Sir,
every day I lift my eyes to the stars
and I lower my knee to the ground.

tomb reflections

Is it night? is it day? hard to say...
Why not me? Why were You hanging there?
Who's fault is it? Mine? Yours? And who cares, anyway?...
Now my plea is in vain, and I feast on despair.

So, what now? You are gone – all is lost.
Anyway, any hope was absurd.
Many said you were crazy, and what rankles the most
is their laughs: they sound true, the truest I've heard.

Forgive me, but I hoped that bolts from on high
Would crash on their heads, on their children, and cattle!
Why no fight from You, no miracle in the sky?
You seemed to just give up well before the battle.

Was it all deceit? When You seemed so true?!
I'll get away from here; I can't bear this load,
I can't stand those who sneer at me, at You.
So, I'll will run to Emmaus, on the evening road.

betrayed

A perfidious light reflects from the oval mirror:
as you cut my soul into thin long stripes,
with the moves of a skilled, sadistic butcher.
With these shards of daylight you seek to ambush me,
between the sorrows of a cold, late afternoon
in an almost forgotten winter,
just like wolves drooling
for the arrival of an innocent deer.
Who the hell invited you here?
Like the years and the days
with their regrets,
you're barging in ready for the kill.
You hide a knife –
cloaked in the double-crossing light
shining through that merciless mirror –
a scalpel perhaps, barely visible,
to drive it deep inside me
for the implacable diminution
of my hope towards despair.
I whisper the words,
broken over millennia,
uttered by the other Betrayed:
Do what you must. Hurry up!

As I fall, I glimpse the mirror:
it's me with the bloody scalpel in my hand!

angel with dewdrops

Cattle horns, maybe of buffalo, laying on the burnt field –
a cadaveric miasma clawing at your nostrils,
defeats the horizon and nails the sun to the top of your head.
Leavened corpses, teeming with rotting life,
decomposing through the broken dirt
like the last gaze of the lusterless eyes
hacked by the dreadful screeching of sandpaper.
Fear prevails to the last drop, the last shred of your life,
a ghastly and vain desperation.
This is a doomed scuffle, and you know it.

But should an angel exist –
a go-between, a substitute in that screeching death –
he will squeeze celestial dewdrops for you to sip,
and then he'll fly you to the shores of the river of life.

let's slay Santa tonight

Our children, precious little darlings
are waiting for Christmas, joyful and sprite –
oh! baby! my darling, my sweetie
let's slay Santa, cut his throat tonight!

In the city, shopwindows are electrically glowing
with Christmas lights flashing luridly bright –
sugar pie, wouldn't it be awesome
to fry Santa on high voltage tonight!

Of all the Christmas trees, let's purchase the biggest!
tie it down with a rope, make it tight –
honeybear, my angel, my pumpkin,
let us hang Santa by his neck, from its branches, tonight!

Old grandma's cooking up a storm
for our Christmas dinner – what a sight!
But if you make your way to the kitchen, my lovely,
please shove Santa into the oven – bake him crispy, tonight.

The fireworks are blasting up in the sky, my treasure…
filling the children with awe and delight.
But you, my gorgeous, get hold of the gun
and blast Santa! Blow his brains, like fireworks, tonight.

And then, my butterfly, once we are sure he's carked it,
we'll tell the children, who'll be sad and contrite,
that, bored to death by stupid toys,
Santa killed himself this Christmas night.

ashes of my stars

My stars are burning;
they are almost ashes.
They waited, hung around, I strung them along
but today they said to me they've had enough.
A stellar suicide was inevitable.
Nothing could change their mind…
I acknowledged my guilt,
I promised them everything under the sun
(what was beyond it, they already owned),
I even promised them their freedom.
Nothing could convince them to stay.
Their last flicker has died and they are gone.
Now I gather their ashes
to put it into a crystal jar.
I play funeral director
for my stars.

abide with us

We're born entwined in agony and love,
blind, helpless, unaware of all the fuss,
a mother's smile through tears is all we crave,
but first, we faintly cry "abide with us".

When with the buds of springtime, bold and bright,
we're picking love, like ruddy flowers through the grass,
and keenly drink the lavishness of life,
we playfully exclaim from time to time "abide with us".

But as the summer comes, with its hot swirling winds
and scatters sometimes diamonds, sometimes brass –
bereft of time, we utter, on the run,
a seldom, an abrupt "abide with us".

And then, when squeezed under the years, we're casting
one longing eye behind, before we pass,
a strange and lonely nightmare, creeping nightly,
imples us whispering with dismay "abide with us".

Abide with us: the sun is setting meekly
over our given time – as ephemeral as the grass;
so, linger please, to break our daily bread,
and through the night, we pray, abide with us.

www.ingramcontent.com/pod-product-compliance
Lightning Source LLC
Chambersburg PA
CBHW032008080426
42735CB00007B/546